KAREN LEE

Vegetarian

Photography by SIMON WHEELER

THE MASTER CHEFS

TED SMART

KAREN LEE is well known in the United States as an author, caterer and teacher, appearing frequently on national and local radio and television shows. She has owned and operated her own cooking school in New York City since 1972, and is noted as a top caterer by the *Zagat Guide*, *New York Magazine* and *New York Times*.

She has written three books on Chinese cooking, and her latest book, *The Occasional Vegetarian* (Warner Books, 1995), is now in its third printing.

Photograph by Frank Grunberg

CONTENTS

The best things and the best
people rise out of separateness.
I'm against an homogenized
society. I want the cream to rise.

ROBERT FROST

INTRODUCTION

When I eat vegetarian I feel wonderful. My weight, blood pressure and cholesterol stay down and my energy stays up.

These are some of my favourite vegetable, grain and pasta recipes, which are low in fat, yet high in flavour. They are easy to assemble, and very versatile: mix and match two or three dishes to make a vegetarian feast, or choose just one as a first course or side dish.

The ingredients are readily available – but if you can't find them, don't be afraid to substitute others. It is more important to be fussy when buying your ingredients: the better they are the tastier – and healthier – the dish will be. Make sure your green vegetables are intensely green, with no trace of brown or yellow. "Was it delivered today?" you might ask. Vegetables lose vitamins and flavour from the moment they are picked.

This is the cooking of the '90s, for people who want live into their 90s. And I mean really living and feeling well. Cooking healthy tasty meals is the best gift you can give yourself, your family and your friends.

GREEN BEAN SALAD
with balsamic vinaigrette

450 G/1 LB GREEN BEANS

3–4 SPRING ONIONS, THINLY SLICED

2 TABLESPOONS CHOPPED FRESH
    DILL

SALAD LEAVES, TO SERVE

BALSAMIC VINAIGRETTE

$\frac{1}{2}$ TEASPOON SALT

$\frac{3}{4}$ TABLESPOON BALSAMIC VINEGAR

$\frac{3}{4}$ TABLESPOON RED WINE VINEGAR

1 TEASPOON DIJON MUSTARD

$\frac{1}{8}$ TEASPOON FRESHLY GROUND
    BLACK PEPPER

3 TABLESPOONS OLIVE OIL

SERVES 4–6

To make the balsamic vinaigrette: dissolve the salt in the vinegars in a screw-topped glass jar. Add the mustard, pepper and olive oil and shake vigorously. The vinaigrette can be kept in the refrigerator for up to 5 days.

Steam the green beans for 3–4 minutes, then plunge them into ice cold water for 2 minutes to stop the cooking and hold the colour. Drain well and trim the stem ends. The beans can be prepared up to 8 hours in advance.

Place the beans in a serving bowl. Add the spring onions, dill and dressing and toss until combined. Serve at once or within 1 hour, on a bed of salad leaves.

SAUTÉED PEPPERS
with garlic and capers

2 RED OR YELLOW PEPPERS, SEEDED
    AND CUT INTO LARGE SQUARES
1½ TABLESPOONS OLIVE OIL
1 LARGE GARLIC CLOVE, SLICED
1 TABLESPOON CAPERS, RINSED AND
    DRAINED
4 TABLESPOONS DRY WHITE WINE
SALT AND FRESHLY GROUND
    BLACK PEPPER

SERVES 2–4

Sauté the peppers in the olive oil over medium heat for about 5–10 minutes or until they soften and are cooked through – it does not matter if they brown slightly. After about 4 minutes, add the garlic and stir occasionally – the garlic should brown slightly.

Add the capers, stir briefly, then, using a slotted spoon, transfer the contents of the pan to a warmed serving dish.

Add the white wine to the pan and stir over low heat to deglaze the pan and reduce the liquid by half. Taste the liquid and adjust the seasoning if required, then pour over the peppers. Serve hot or at room temperature, with warm bread or over rice or pasta.

GREEK SALAD

⅓ TEASPOON SALT

1 TABLESPOON LEMON JUICE

2½ TABLESPOONS OLIVE OIL

⅛ TEASPOON FRESHLY GROUND
   BLACK PEPPER

¼ TEASPOON DRIED OREGANO

50 G/2 OZ BLACK OLIVES

1 SMALL RED ONION, SLICED

2 TABLESPOONS CHOPPED FRESH
   PARSLEY

3–4 FIRM, RIPE, WELL-FLAVOURED
   TOMATOES, CUT INTO CHUNKS

85 G/3 OZ FETA CHEESE, DICED

1 HEAD OF COS LETTUCE, TORN
   INTO PIECES

SERVES 3–4

Dissolve the salt in the lemon juice in the bottom of a salad bowl. Add the olive oil, pepper, oregano, olives, onion, parsley, tomatoes and cheese; toss gently and leave to marinate for at least 15 minutes or up to 1 hour.

Add the lettuce to the salad bowl; toss and serve immediately.

WHITE BEAN BRUSCHETTA

1 TEASPOON CHOPPED FRESH
   ROSEMARY LEAVES

1½ TABLESPOONS OLIVE OIL

3 GARLIC CLOVES, SLIGHTLY
   CRUSHED

BRAISED WHITE BEANS (PAGE 29),
   NOT DRAINED, OR
     1 x 400 G/14 OZ CAN
     HARICOT OR CANNELLINI BEANS,
     DRAINED

1 TEASPOON BALSAMIC VINEGAR

⅛ TEASPOON CHILLI FLAKES OR
   CAYENNE PEPPER

SALT AND FRESHLY GROUND
   BLACK PEPPER

1 ITALIAN-STYLE LOAF

SERVES 6–8

Mix the chopped rosemary with ½ tablespoon of the olive oil and leave to infuse for at least 30 minutes.

In a small saucepan over the lowest possible heat – or over a heat-diffusing mat if you cannot get a really low heat – cook the garlic in the remaining olive oil for 20–30 minutes or until the garlic has softened and browned; turn the garlic cloves every so often.

Using a fork, mash the softened garlic in the olive oil, then add to the white beans, together with the rosemary and its oil, balsamic vinegar and chilli or cayenne. Mash the beans slightly, using a fork or potato masher. The beans can be prepared up to 8 hours in advance.

To serve, reheat the beans. Taste and adjust the seasoning if required. Slice the bread 1 cm/ ½ inch thick and toast on both sides. Cut each slice in half and spoon the beans on to the bread.

LINGUINE WITH TOMATO SAUCE
and sautéed aubergine

450 G/1 LB AUBERGINE, CUT INTO
   THIN STRIPS

2 TEASPOONS SALT

5 TABLESPOONS OLIVE OIL

4 GARLIC CLOVES, CHOPPED

TOMATO SAUCE (PAGE 29)

4 TABLESPOONS DRY WHITE WINE

¼ TEASPOON FRESHLY GROUND
   BLACK PEPPER

¼ TEASPOON CAYENNE PEPPER

1 TABLESPOON CHOPPED FRESH
   OREGANO, OR 1 TEASPOON
   DRIED OREGANO

325 G/12 OZ DRIED LINGUINE OR
   SPAGHETTI

85–125 G/3–4 OZ PARMESAN
   CHEESE, GRATED

SERVES 3–4

Place the aubergine strips in a bowl with 1 teaspoon of the salt. Toss to mix and leave for 1 hour.

Rinse the aubergine in cold water, then drain and pat dry.

Place a large, heavy-based saucepan over high heat, add 1 tablespoon of the olive oil and reduce the heat to low. Add the garlic and sauté for 2 minutes or until it has just begun to turn golden. Add the tomato sauce, wine, black and cayenne pepper and oregano; simmer for 3 minutes.

Cook the pasta in a large saucepan of boiling water with 1 teaspoon of salt for 7–9 minutes or until just tender. Drain, reserving the cooking water.

Heat a large frying pan over high heat, add the remaining olive oil and sauté the aubergine for about 5 minutes or until crisp.

Bring the sauce to a simmer and add the pasta, aubergine and 4 tablespoons of the pasta cooking water. Toss over low heat for about 1 minute. Add the cheese, mix briefly and serve at once.

FARFALLE WITH PORCINI
and tomato sauce

40 G/1½ OZ DRIED PORCINI
    MUSHROOMS (CEPS)
1 TABLESPOON OLIVE OIL
1 TABLESPOON CHOPPED GARLIC
2–3 SHALLOTS, CHOPPED
½ RECIPE TOMATO SAUCE (PAGE 29)
1 TABLESPOON CREAM
1 TABLESPOON MILK
2 TABLESPOONS CHOPPED FRESH
    FLAT-LEAF PARSLEY
1 TEASPOON SALT
225 G/8 OZ DRIED FARFALLE
    (BOW-TIE PASTA)
50 G/2 OZ PARMESAN CHEESE,
    GRATED

SERVES 2

Place the ceps in a bowl and cover with 250 ml/8 fl oz cold water. Leave to soak for 30 minutes or until soft. Squeeze the mushrooms over the bowl, then cut into dice. Strain the liquid into a small saucepan and boil until reduced to 4 tablespoons. Set aside.

Place a frying pan over medium heat, add the olive oil and reduce the heat to low. Add the garlic and sauté for about 2 minutes. Add the shallots and porcini and sauté for a further 2 minutes or until the shallots are soft. Add the tomato sauce, simmer for 1 minute, then add the cream, milk and parsley and simmer for a further 1 minute.

The sauce can be prepared in advance and stored in the refrigerator for up to 3 days.

To serve, cook the pasta in a large saucepan of boiling water with the salt for 9–10 minutes or until just tender. Drain well.

Bring the sauce to a simmer and add the porcini liquid. Add the pasta and toss over low heat for about 1 minute. Add the cheese, mix briefly and serve at once.

CREAMY POLENTA
with three cheeses

500 ML/16 FL OZ SKIMMED MILK

500 ML/16 FL OZ WATER

1½ TEASPOONS SALT

¼ TEASPOON GROUND WHITE
  PEPPER

225 G/8 OZ COARSE CORNMEAL
  (POLENTA)

175 G/6 OZ MIXED PARMESAN,
  CHEDDAR AND GOATS' CHEESE,
  GRATED OR CHOPPED

SERVES 6–8

Bring the milk and water to the
boil in a heavy-based saucepan.
Add the salt and pepper, then add
the cornmeal in a slow and steady
stream, stirring continuously until
all the cornmeal is absorbed, about
3 minutes.

Reduce the heat to very low
and, using a large wooden spoon
or spatula, stir the cornmeal in a
figure-of-eight motion almost
constantly for 18–20 minutes (or
less if using quick-cooking
polenta). The polenta is done when
it adheres to itself and pulls away
from the sides of the pan.

Remove from the heat, add the
cheese and stir until melted, about
1–2 minutes.

Serve piping hot. Alternatively,
place in a buttered or oiled
heatproof dish, leave to cool, then
cover and store in the refrigerator.
To serve, brush with butter or olive
oil and place under a hot grill for
2–3 minutes or until lightly
browned. Then bake in a preheated
oven at 190°C/375°F/Gas Mark 5
for 5–10 minutes.

THREE-GRAIN FRIED RICE

85 G/3 OZ SHORT-GRAIN BROWN
RICE
85 G/3 OZ BROWN SWEET RICE
(AVAILABLE FROM HEALTH FOOD
SHOPS), OR BASMATI RICE
(BROWN OR WHITE)
85 G/3 OZ WHOLE WHEAT BERRIES
1½ TABLESPOONS PEANUT OIL
ABOUT 325 G/12 OZ MIXED
VEGETABLES, SUCH AS RED AND
YELLOW PEPPERS, MANGETOUT,
SPRING ONIONS, CARROTS, CUT
INTO MATCHSTICKS
1 TABLESPOON SOY SAUCE
½ TABLESPOON OYSTER SAUCE
(OPTIONAL)
1 TABLESPOON SESAME SEEDS,
ROASTED (PAGE 30)

SERVES 4

Wash all the rice and wheat berries
and leave to drain. While they are
draining, bring 375 ml/12 fl oz
water to a rolling boil over high
heat. Add the grains and return to
the boil. Stir, cover, reduce the heat
to low and simmer for 30 minutes.

Remove the pan from the heat
and leave to stand for 30 minutes.
Spread the grains on a plate; when
cool, cover and refrigerate for at
least 3 hours or up to 3 days.

Place a wok over high heat
until it begins to smoke. Add 1
tablespoon of the oil, swirl it
around the wok, then add the cold
grains. Reduce the heat and stir-fry
for about 2–3 minutes, pushing
down with the back of a spatula so
that the grains scorch. Remove the
grains from the wok.

Return the wok to a high heat,
add the remaining oil and the
vegetables and stir-fry for 2–3
minutes. Return the grains to the
wok with the soy and oyster
sauces, and stir-fry for 1–2
minutes. Serve at once, topped
with the roasted sesame seeds.

CRISPY BROCCOLI

½ HEAD OF BROCCOLI
2 TABLESPOONS OLIVE OIL
⅓ TEASPOON SALT
2 TABLESPOONS SLICED GARLIC
⅛ TEASPOON CAYENNE PEPPER

SERVES 2–4

Wash and drain the broccoli. Cut off and discard about 5 cm/ 2 inches of the stem. Peel the remaining stem, then slice into 1 cm/½ inch thick pieces; when you come to the florets, break them up.

Place a frying pan over medium heat, add the olive oil and salt and heat for 1 minute, then reduce the heat to low, add the garlic and sauté for 2 minutes.

Add the broccoli and cayenne pepper and toss to mix well. Sauté over medium heat for 5 minutes, tossing occasionally until the broccoli is cooked through but still a little crunchy. Serve hot or at room temperature.

BRAISED GREENS

325 G/12 OZ MIXED GREENS, SUCH
AS KALE, SWISS CHARD
1½ TABLESPOONS OLIVE OIL
⅓ TEASPOON SALT
2 GARLIC CLOVES, CHOPPED
1½ LEEKS, CUT INTO 1 CM/½ INCH
PIECES
ABOUT 125 ML/4 FL OZ VEGETABLE
STOCK (PAGE 28)
¼ TEASPOON FRESHLY GROUND
BLACK PEPPER

SERVES 2–4

Wash and drain the greens. Remove and discard any tough kale stems. Cut the greens into 2.5 cm/1 inch pieces, keeping the Swiss chard stems separate.

Place a wok or large saucepan over high heat for 1 minute, then reduce the heat to very low and add the olive oil, salt, garlic and leeks; sauté for about 10 minutes. The garlic and leeks should not burn, so use a heat-diffusing mat if you cannot get a really low heat.

Add the stock and bring to the boil. If using Swiss chard, add the stems, cover and cook for 3–4 minutes, then add the leaves, cover and cook for a further 6–10 minutes, stirring until slightly wilted. Season to taste with the pepper. Serve hot or at room temperature. Do not reheat.

THE BASICS

VEGETABLE STOCK

8 LITRES/14 PINTS WATER
125 G/4 OZ LENTILS OR CHICKPEAS
GREEN PART OF 4–6 LEEKS, OR 2
    WHOLE LEEKS, ROUGHLY
    CHOPPED
2 LARGE ONIONS, QUARTERED
2 CARROTS AND/OR 2 PARSNIPS,
    ROUGHLY CHOPPED
8 STICKS OF CELERY, ROUGHLY
    CHOPPED
1 PARSLEY ROOT (OPTIONAL),
    GREEN PART DISCARDED,
    ROUGHLY CHOPPED
STEMS FROM 1 BUNCH OF PARSLEY,
    ROUGHLY CHOPPED
50 G/2 OZ MUSHROOM STEMS, OR
    2 TABLESPOONS DRIED
    MUSHROOMS
4 SPRIGS OF THYME
2 BAY LEAVES
10 BLACK PEPPERCORNS
1 TABLESPOON MIRIN OR PORT
    (OPTIONAL)

**MAKES ABOUT 4 LITRES/
7 PINTS**
Put all the ingredients, except the
mirin or port, into a stock pot.
Bring to the boil over high heat,
then adjust the heat to maintain a
fast simmer for 1 hour.

Strain, discard the vegetables
and add the mirin or port.

The stock can be stored in the
refrigerator for up to 5 days or
frozen for up to 6 months.

★ For a more intense flavour,
return the strained stock to the pot
and reduce it by boiling for about
1 hour.
★ If you don't have every
ingredient listed, do without.
I sometimes include a few of the
outside leaves of a head of lettuce.
★ For a great spa drink – with zero
fat – leave out the mirin or port
and place the hot stock in a mug
with a few drops of umeboshi
vinegar (Japanese plum vinegar).

TOMATO SAUCE

2 TABLESPOONS OLIVE OIL
1 LEEK, DICED
1.5 KG/3 LB VERY RIPE PLUM
    TOMATOES, OR 2 X 400 G/14 OZ
    CANS PLUM TOMATOES
1 TEASPOON SUGAR
1 TEASPOON SALT
½ TEASPOON FRESHLY GROUND
    BLACK PEPPER

**MAKES ABOUT 750 ML/
1¼ PINTS**

Heat a large frying pan, add the oil
and leek and sauté for about 5
minutes or until the leek softens.

If using fresh tomatoes, dice
them without peeling; if using
canned tomatoes, crush them
together with their juice. Add the
tomatoes and juice to the frying
pan, with the sugar, salt and
pepper. Bring to the boil over high
heat, stir well, then simmer over
low heat, uncovered, for 30–45
minutes or until the sauce has
reduced by half.

The sauce can be stored in the
refrigerator for 1 week or frozen
for up to 6 months.

BRAISED WHITE BEANS

225 G/8 OZ DRIED WHITE BEANS
500 ML/16 FL OZ WATER
1 BAY LEAF
⅛ TEASPOON FRESHLY GROUND
    BLACK PEPPER
1 CARROT, CUT IN HALF
1 LARGE ONION, QUARTERED
2 GARLIC CLOVES
A FEW SPRIGS OF PARSLEY AND
    THYME (OR ½ TEASPOON DRIED
    THYME), TIED IN A PIECE OF
    MUSLIN
1 TEASPOON SALT

**MAKES ABOUT 600 ML/
1 PINT**

Wash the beans, then leave to soak
for 6–8 hours or overnight.

Pour off the water and place
the soaked beans in a saucepan
with a tight-fitting lid. Add the
measured water, bay leaf, pepper,
carrot, onion, garlic and parsley and
thyme in the muslin.

Cover the pan, bring to the boil
over high heat, then simmer gently
for 1 hour. Add the salt during the
last 15 minutes of cooking time.

Remove the herbs and
vegetables and serve the beans hot
or at room temperature.

TECHNIQUES AND TIPS

Don't throw away vitamins: save all steaming and boiling water from vegetables to use as a substitute for stock.

When washing leafy greens for salads, fill a bowl with cold water (add a few ice cubes to make it even colder), then submerge the leaves; this prevents them from being bruised by the force of the water. Lift out and spin dry.

To lessen the strong taste of red onion, chop or slice, then soak in iced water with a good squeeze of lemon juice for 30 minutes. The same technique gives chicory a sweeter taste.

Always allow rice to 'relax' before serving. When the rice is cooked, turn off the heat and leave the pan with the lid on for 15–30 minutes. (If using an electric burner, remove the pan from the heat source.) This improves the consistency and means that the rice doesn't stick to the bottom of the pan.

The secret of perfect fried rice is to use cooked cold rice. You can use any variety of rice, or a combination of varieties.

To roast sesame seeds, heat a wok or heavy-based frying pan over high heat for 1 minute. Reduce the heat to low and add about 4 tablespoons sesame seeds. Roast for 5–10 minutes or until the sesame seeds are golden brown. They can be stored in a lidded glass jar in the refrigerator for 1 month. Sesame seeds are a good source of calcium.

THE MASTER CHEFS

SOUPS
ARABELLA BOXER

MEZE, TAPAS AND ANTIPASTI
AGLAIA KREMEZI

PASTA SAUCES
GORDON RAMSAY

RISOTTO
MICHELE SCICOLONE

SALADS
CLARE CONNERY

MEDITERRANEAN
ANTONY WORRALL THOMPSON

VEGETABLES
PAUL GAYLER

LUNCHES
ALASTAIR LITTLE

COOKING FOR TWO
RICHARD OLNEY

FISH
RICK STEIN

CHICKEN
BRUNO LOUBET

SUPPERS
VALENTINA HARRIS

THE MAIN COURSE
ROGER VERGÉ

ROASTS
JANEEN SARLIN

WILD FOOD
ROWLEY LEIGH

PACIFIC
JILL DUPLEIX

CURRIES
PAT CHAPMAN

HOT AND SPICY
PAUL AND JEANNE RANKIN

THAI
JACKI PASSMORE

CHINESE
YAN-KIT SO

VEGETARIAN
KAREN LEE

DESSERTS
MICHEL ROUX

CAKES
CAROLE WALTER

COOKIES
ELINOR KLIVANS

THE MASTER CHEFS

This edition produced for The Book People Ltd,

Hall Wood Avenue, Haydock, St Helens WA11 9UL

Text © copyright 1996 Karen Lee

Karen Lee has asserted her right to be

identified as the Author of this Work.

Photographs © copyright 1996 Simon Wheeler

First published in 1996 by

WEIDENFELD & NICOLSON

THE ORION PUBLISHING GROUP

ORION HOUSE

5 UPPER ST MARTIN'S LANE

LONDON WC2H 9EA

All rights reserved. No part of this publication may be
reproduced, stored in a retrieval system, or
transmitted in any form or by any means, electronic,
mechanical or otherwise, without prior permission of
the copyright holder.

British Library Cataloguing-in-Publication data

A catalogue record for this book is available

from the British Library.

ISBN 0 297 83646 3

DESIGNED BY THE SENATE

EDITOR MAGGIE RAMSAY

FOOD STYLIST JOY DAVIES